The Complete Haiku 1974-2024

Alex Telman

Published by Alex Telman, 2024.

THE COMPLETE HAIKU 1974-2024

First edition. September 16, 2024.

ISBN: 979-8230731115

Written by Alex Telman.

Table of Contents

Dedication To Basho

Ancient paths whisper,
Basho’s pen in moonlit shade—
time's echo in ink
Basho's voice guides still,
echoes in each line I write—
moonlight in my verse

Introduction

Alex Telman stands as one of Australia's most esteemed poets, celebrated for his mastery of the haiku form. With a career spanning five decades, Telman's work embodies the delicate precision and depth that define this timeless genre.

In *Telman: The Complete Haiku 1974-2024*, Telman offers a comprehensive collection of his life's work, meticulously curated into thematic groups of five haiku each. This volume not only showcases his extensive output but also reveals the evolution of his craft, from his early explorations to his latest reflections.

As a writer for whom English is a second language, Telman's obsessive pursuit of linguistic precision and his quest for the perfect word have culminated in haiku that resonate with profound clarity. His dedication to capturing the essence of fleeting moments reflects a relentless commitment to the art form.

Telman: The Complete Haiku 1974-2024 is set to be an indispensable resource for poetry enthusiasts and scholars alike. This collection stands as a testament to Telman's influence and is destined to remain a defining example of the haiku tradition for future generations.

Feeding pigeons as a young boy

Alex Telman, age 3

1
Young boy spreads his hands,
pigeons gather in a swirl—
innocence in flight
2
In morning's soft light,
a boy scatters crumbs to birds—
pigeons' gentle peck
3
Small hands hold the seed,

pigeons flutter in delight—
childhood's quiet joy

4

Boy and pigeons meet,
crumbs fall like soft autumn leaves—
serenity shared

5

Feeding pigeons' dance,
a boy's laughter fills the air—
moments of pure peace

Cherry Blossoms

1
Cherry blossoms fall—
a lone bird lifts from the branch,
spring's breath fades away
2
Soft rain on petals,
a child's whispering dreams—
cherry trees sigh gently
3
Moonlight through the trees,
cherry blossoms gently drift—
night holds its breath still
4
Under blossoms' shade,
a worn path leads to silence—
spring's quiet journey
5
Blossoms on the breeze,
each petal a fleeting thought—
spring's soft farewell kiss

Moonlight on Water

1
Moonlight on the pond—
a single ripple whispers,
night breathes in stillness
2
Silver waves tremble,
moonlight dances with the breeze—
night's soft, fleeting touch
3
Moon's glow on the lake,
ripples trace a silent path—
water holds the night
4
Moon's path on still pond,
clouds drift in its gentle light—
night's embrace is calm
5
Under moon's soft gaze,
water mirrors ancient stars—
quiet night unfolds

Sledding with my father

Poland, 1959

1
Snow whispers beneath,
boy and father sledding down—
laughter in the cold
2
On a snowy hill,
father and son glide swift—
winter's joyous flight
3
Father's steady hand,
young boy's gleeful shouts on snow—
winter's warm embrace
4
Sled tracks in the snow,

father and son ride the crest—
echoes of delight

5

In the frosty air,
a boy's laughter trails behind—
sledding with my dad

First snowfall of winter

1
First snow softly falls—
one footprint lost in white drifts,
winter's breath is still
2
Bare branches turn white,
first snow whispers in the dusk—
winter's breath is cold
3
Snowflakes kiss the earth,
a quiet world now adorned—
first snow's gentle touch
4
Snow drifts on the fence,
each post dons a winter coat—
first snowfall's still song
5
Morning's hush reveals,
first snow cloaks the world in white—
breath hangs in the chill

A lone wolf howling

1
Moonlight on the ridge,
a lone wolf's howl shatters still—
winter's breath lingers
2
Silent woods embrace,
a wolf's lone cry breaks the night—
darkness holds its breath
3
In the still night air,
a wolf's mournful howl rises—
stars blink in reply
4
Snow cloaks the dark land,
a lone wolf's call pierces still—
night's cold whispers on
5
Howl beneath the stars,
a lone wolf fades into night—
winter's voice alone

Early morning fog

1
Fog veils the still pond—
morning light breaks the silence,
trees emerge from gray
2
Early fog drifts in,
whispers through the quiet field—
dawn's breath softly stirs
3
Mist cloaks the old path,
a distant crow's faint echo—
day's breath holds its peace
4
Fog drapes the still dawn,
mountains fade in soft embrace—
morning's quiet veil
5
In the fog's stillness,
morning light cuts through the haze—
world stirs from a dream

Falling leaves in autumn

1
Leaves drift through the air,
autumn whispers softly—
a quiet dance ends
2
Falling leaves descend,
a single leaf lands gently—
wind's last sigh of fall
3
Crisp leaves drift away,
blanket of red on the path—
autumn's fleeting touch
4
Golden leaves cascade,
dusk stirs with a gentle breeze—
fall's brief, soft embrace
5
Amid falling leaves,
a lone crow's call breaks the dusk—
autumn's silent end

A river's gentle flow

1
River's quiet flow,
sunlight dances on its path—
whispers through the reeds
2
Soft current hums low,
a lone leaf drifts with the tide—
day's calm reflection
3
Gentle river glides,
mountains shadow in its wake—
stillness fills the air
4
Ripples kiss the shore,
river's flow in twilight's hush—
night's embrace begins
5
On the river's path,
a dragonfly rests lightly—
time moves with the stream

Rain on a rooftop

1
Rain taps on the roof—
a soft rhythm in the night,
silence deepens still
2
Raindrops on the tiles,
a gentle song in the dusk—
night's quiet embrace
3
Rain patterns on slate,
roof weeps softly in the gray—
each drop a whisper
4
Old roof sighs beneath rain,
world draped in quiet stillness—
warmth within the storm
5
Rain on the rooftop,
a rhythm soothes the dark—
night wrapped in its sound

A lone star in the sky

1
Lone star in the night,
a beacon in the vast dark—
silent guide above
2
One star pierces night,
cold light in the endless sky—
solitude's soft glow
3
In the quiet night,
a single star gently shines—
the sky's gentle pulse
4
A lone star glimmers,
framed by the vast dark expanse—
night's solitary eye
5
One star lights the sky,
an ancient, silent witness—
night's quiet whisper

The scent of pine needles

1
Pine needles' soft scent,
whispers through the ancient pines—
a breath of old woods
2
Among pine branches,
scent of fallen needles drifts—
autumn's quiet breath
3
Fresh pine in the breeze,
needles scent the morning air—
forest's gentle touch
4
Under pine's green shade,
scent of needles mingles with sun—
a moment of calm
5
Pine needles rustle,
a hint of forest perfume—
nature's deep exhale

A deserted beach

1
Empty shoreline waits,
waves whisper to the still sand—
quiet solitude
2
Footprints fade away,
ocean's edge breathes calm and still—
a lone gull drifts by
3
Deserted beach sighs,
sea breeze stirs the empty dusk—
tide's soft, distant song
4
Shells scattered on sand,
a distant wave's gentle kiss—
deserted shore waits
5
Under pale sky's hush,
waves curl on a lonely shore—
beach dreams in stillness

A blooming cactus

1
Cactus blooms at dawn,
fragile flowers pierce the spines—
desert's gentle touch
2
In desert's harsh light,
a cactus blooms defiantly—
petals blush in sun
3
Among arid stones,
a cactus opens its heart—
blossoms in the dry
4
Cactus flower blooms,
bright against the barren earth—
spring's gift to the dry
5
Spiny arms outstretched,
a single bloom's quiet grace—
desert's fleeting jewel

A fresh breeze in spring

1
Spring breeze through the pines,
whispers stir the new green leaves—
winter's breath retreats
2
A fresh spring breeze blows,
petals flutter in the sun—
soft dance of the blooms
3
Gentle spring breeze stirs,
over fields of budding grass—
earth awakens new
4
Spring breeze through the pines,
carries scents of blossoms fresh—
nature's gentle sigh
5
Under spring's soft breath,
a lone cherry petal drifts—
fresh air's quiet kiss

A boy and his puppy

Alex and Anika, 1972

1
In the soft sunlight,
boy and puppy tumble play—
laughter fills the air
2
Puppy's playful bark,
young boy's tender touch and smile—
joy in every bound
3
Collie pup and boy,
chasing shadows in the light—
friendship's joyful chase
4
On a grassy hill,
boy and puppy's happy romp—
innocence and joy
5

Tender Anika,
boy's gentle hand soothes her fur—
warmth in summer's glow

A bustling city street

1
City street hums loud,
neon lights blur through the crowd—
night's restless pulse
2
In the street's loud rush,
a lone pigeon pecks at crumbs—
silence in the storm
3
Rain on pavement glints,
footsteps echo through the din—
a brief, soft respite
4
Crowds surge and recede,
yellow taxis weave like bees—
urban life breathes
5
Street vendors call out,
voices merge in city hum—
a fleeting stillness

An old wooden bridge

1
Old bridge spans the stream,
weathered planks creak with each step—
echoes of the past
2
Autumn leaves drift by,
floating on the old bridge's span—
memories in flow
3
Mist cloaks the old bridge,
ancient beams embrace the dawn—
silence spans the creek
4
Rain drips from the bridge,
wood soaks up the morning light—
a path through stillness
5
Under moonlight's gaze,
the old bridge rests, timeless, still—
water's gentle flow

A sleeping cat

1
Sunlight warms the fur,
a sleeping cat's gentle purr—
dreams in quiet light
2
Curled in soft repose,
a sleeping cat's breath is slow—
peace within the day
3
On the windowsill,
a cat dreams in dappled light—
day's warmth enfolds
4
Silent through the night,
a cat sleeps beneath moonlight—
dreams guarded by peace
5
Beneath soft quilt's warmth,
a cat's breath rises and falls—
stillness fills the house

A crackling fireplace

1
Logs crackle and glow,
warmth dances in the hearth's light—
winter's gentle roar
2
Flames leap and whisper,
the fireplace hums its tune—
night's cozy embrace
3
Crackling firelight,
shadows dance upon the walls—
stillness warms the room
4
Embers softly glow,
crackling through the quiet night—
fire's tender sigh
5
In the hearth's warm glow,
each log bursts with fleeting light—
winter's crackling song

A mountain peak

1
Mountain peak in mist,
silent beneath morning light—
clouds drift at its feet
2
Snow crowns the summit,
a lone eagle circles high—
whispers touch the sky
3
Above the world's reach,
the mountain peak stands serene—
a silent sentinel
4
On the peak's still edge,
wind whispers through ancient stone—
cold breath of the sky
5
Peak pierces the dawn,
crags etched in the morning light—
stillness in the heights

Sunlight through trees

1
Sunlight filters down,
leaves whisper in golden beams—
forest's quiet grace
2
Morning sun breaks through,
dappled light on ancient trunks—
shadows dance on leaves
3
Sunlight through the boughs,
patterns shift on the forest floor—
day's gentle touch
4
Golden beams cascade,
through the canopy's embrace—
whispers of the dawn
5
Sunlight streaks through trees,
a mosaic on the ground—
stillness in the light

A flickering candle

1
Candle's flame dances,
shadows waltz on quiet walls—
night's fleeting embrace
2
In the stillness, light
flickers with a soft murmur—
whispers in the dark
3
A lone candle burns,
its flame sways in silent song—
evening's gentle pulse
4
Flickering candle,
flame quivers in the cool air—
dreams waver and fade
5
Soft light flickers low,
casting warmth in darkened room—
stillness warms the night

A field of wildflowers

1
Breeze caresses blooms—
wildflowers bend and whisper,
secrets in the wind
2
Morning light unfolds,
a sea of blooms breathes softly,
color's quiet waltz
3
Petals catch the dusk,
a chorus of fading hues—
sun's final embrace
4
Under vast blue skies,
wildflowers dream of rainfall,
earth's gentle sighs blend
5
Bees hum in twilight,
wildflowers sway in rhythm—
nature's evening song

A rainy day in summer

1
Summer rain descends—
whispers on the thirsty earth,
cool touch in the dusk
2
Clouds veil the soft sky,
raindrops dance on summer leaves,
stillness in the storm
3
In summer rain,
cicadas' muted songs—
leaves shimmer with life
4
Ripples on the pond,
summer's warm tears fall and blend—
rain's gentle embrace
5
Umbrellas bloom,
summer showers drape the street—
laughter in the mist

A quiet library

1
Whispers of old tomes,
silence drapes the wooden shelves—
knowledge breathes in peace
2
Dust on ancient spines,
sunlight filters through the glass—
pages rest in still
3
Echoes softly tread,
footsteps lost among the shelves—
books hold their secrets
4
A gentle rustle,
pages turn in quiet rooms—
thoughts drift on still air
5
In hushed stillness,
words sleep within their bindings—
time pauses in calm

A quiet library

1
Silent wooden shelves,
dust settles on forgotten
spines as time drifts on
2
Soft light on old pages,
a whisper in the still air—
stories rest in peace
3
Ink's quiet refuge,
words nestle in the calm dusk—
thoughts linger on shelves
4
Shadows on the floor,
gentle rustle of pages—
silence holds its breath
5
In the quiet room,
a lone chair creaks softly—
books hum in stillness

A serene temple

1
Stillness in the shrine,
incense drifts through quiet air—
echoes of calm grace
2
Stone steps worn by time,
bamboo whispers in the breeze—
temple's tranquil heart
3
Moss on ancient stones,
a chant drifts on the still breeze—
serenity blooms
4
Golden light descends,
shadows dance on tranquil walls—
peace fills the temple
5
In temple's hush,
a bell's ring fades to stillness—
time pauses in grace

A drifting cloud

1
Drifting cloud drifts by,
a whisper across the sky—
echoes of the breeze
2
White cloud drifts so slow,
painting dreams upon the blue—
sky's fleeting canvas
3
In a sea of blue,
a drifting cloud's silent path—
time floats on the wind
4
Soft cloud drifts apart,
shadows chase across the hills—
whispers of the sky
5
Lonely cloud drifts free,
unburdened by the sun's gaze—
wanderer of air

The first light of dawn

1
First light touches trees,
dawn's whisper on the still air—
shadows gently fade
2
Horizon blushes,
morning light breaks the stillness—
night's veil slowly lifts
3
Dew on quiet leaves,
first light spills across the field—
day's breath stirs the grass
4
In dawn's chill, a bird
breaks the silence with its song—
sunrise warms the sky
5
Mist dissolves in light,
first rays dance upon the stream—
day awakens soft

Mother and pusher 1957

Mother pushing Alex, 1956

1
Morning sun on wheels,
young boy waves from the stroller—
mother's gentle stride
2
Old stroller glides on,
mother's soft steps, a boy's laugh—
vintage daydreams bloom
3
In spring's cool morning,

mother pushes the old stroller—
boy's eyes wide with wonder
4
Spring's gentle breeze flows,
mother and son stroll in sync—
stroller's quiet path
5
Boy in stroller's seat,
mother's hands guide through the years—
memories in stride

A rustling autumn path

1
Leaves rustle and fall,
scattered on the autumn path—
footsteps softly tread
2
Crimson leaves descend,
a golden carpet below—
autumn's quiet trail
3
Winding through the woods,
rustling leaves in autumn's breeze—
whispers of the past
4
Bare branches reach high,
rustling leaves on the cool path—
autumn's fleeting breath
5
Path through the still woods,
rustling leaves and fading light—
autumn's soft exhale

A hummingbird at a feeder

1
Hummingbird hovers,
wings a blur at the bright feeder—
nectar's fleeting dance
2
Bright feathers flutter,
a jewel rests at the feeder—
sweet sip in stillness
3
In the summer breeze,
hummingbird sips from the feeder—
delicate rhythm
4
Sunlight on still wings,
hummingbird drinks from the feeder—
momentary pause
5
Hovering so still,
hummingbird's hum at dawn—
nectar's quiet song

A gentle snowfall

1
Snow whispers softly,
blanketing the silent ground—
winter's gentle touch
2
Snowflakes drift on air,
a quiet dance in twilight—
stillness fills the world
3
In fading twilight,
snow falls in delicate drifts—
winter's breath of white
4
Soft snow on the pines,
each branch holds its quiet grace—
silence deepens still
5
Evening's hush falls,
gentle snowflakes kiss the earth—
night wraps in soft white

A sand dune in the desert

1
Lonely sand dune stands,
a crest in the endless sea—
whispers of the wind
2
Golden dune curves high,
shadows play in shifting light—
desert's quiet grace
3
Under blazing sun,
a lone dune shifts with the breeze—
time's soft mark is made
4
Waves of sand unfold,
dune's silhouette at twilight—
stillness in the heat
5
In the desert's hush,
a sand dune's shadow lengthens—
heat dances with dusk

A shimmering lake

1
Sunlight on still lake,
thousand sparkles gently dance—
water's soft embrace
2
Shimmering lake lies,
mirroring the sky's calm hues—
daydreams on still waves
3
Breezes stir the glass,
ripples dance on the lake's sheen—
silence in the light
4
Moonlight on the lake,
silver threads weave through the night—
whispers of the dark
5
Dawn on the lake's face,
gentle ripples catch the light—
morning's quiet song

A lone fisherman

1
Lone fisherman waits,
stillness on the morning lake—
line drifts through the mist
2
In early light,
a single boat drifts on calm—
fisherman's quiet quest
3
At dawn's soft glow,
fisherman's shadow stretches—
ripples touch the shore
4
By the quiet stream,
a lone fisherman's patience—
daybreak's gentle pull
5
Evening's calm falls,
fisherman's silhouette still—
night wraps the quiet lake

Mother at the snow

Mother, 1955 Zakopane, Poland

1
Snowflakes kiss her cheeks,
mother dreams of tiny steps—
child yet to be born
2
In winter's soft hush,
mother wanders through the snow—
cradling hopes unseen
3
Snow drifts on the ground,

mother feels the future's chill—
empty cradle waits
4
Silent snow descends,
mother's gaze soft with pure dreams—
a child's first snowfall
5
Winter's quiet falls,
mother's heart warms to the snow—
waiting for small feet

A snowy mountain pass

1
Whispers on the wind,
snow-clad peaks embrace the dawn—
a lone crow alights
2
Snowflakes kiss the pass,
ancient pines bow to the chill—
breath of winter's hush
3
Footsteps through deep snow,
silent path in moonlit calm—
shadow guides the way
4
Frost on jagged stones,
mountain breath in swirling mists—
a lone fox retreats
5
Icicles hanging,
fractured light on snow's still face—
winter's quiet song

The chirping of crickets

1
Summer night whispers—
crickets weave their ancient song,
moonlight's tender dance
2
In the still night air,
crickets hum their twilight tune,
stars listen with calm
3
Quiet forest edge,
crickets call through shadowed trees,
nature's soft murmur
4
Beneath the old oak,
crickets chirp in rhythmic grace,
time's gentle heartbeat
5
Autumn's chill descends,
crickets' songs grow faint and slow,
leaves drift through the dusk

A misty morning

1
Misty morning veil—
fog drapes the quiet valley,
whispers touch the dawn
2
In dawn's soft embrace,
mist clings to the sleeping field,
pale shapes drift away
3
Through the fogged pines' hush,
ancient trees wear misty veils,
silence breathes anew
4
Morning fog unfolds,
cradling the world in gray,
dreams dissolve with light
5
Dawn's soft mist unfurls—
the river's whisper hidden,
daybreak's gentle sigh

An old oak tree

1
Ancient oak stands still—
gnarled limbs reach for the pale sky,
whispers of the past
2
Beneath old oak's shade,
time's stories carved in its bark,
leaves drift to the ground
3
Weathered oak endures,
silhouetted against dusk,
roots embrace the past
4
In autumn's stillness,
old oak's leaves fall one by one,
echoes in the breeze
5
Winter frost descends—
bare branches of the old oak,
silence holds its breath

A fresh cup of tea

1
Steam rises from the cup—
morning warmth begins anew,
tea's gentle embrace
2
In dawn's quiet light,
fresh tea steeps in porcelain,
peace unfolds in scent
3
Tea's warm breath ascends,
cradled in the morning still,
sips of calm delight
4
Ceramic whispers,
fresh tea swirls in early light,
moments steep in calm
5
First sip of the day—
tea's essence stirs the senses,
sunlight through the steam

A child's laughter

1
Breezes catch their song—
a child's laughter spills bright,
echoes in twilight
2
Sunlit field alive,
a child's laughter dances free,
flowers sway with joy
3
Underneath the oak,
child's laughter fills the still air,
leaves rustle softly
4
In spring's gentle warmth,
laughter rings through blooming fields,
joy spills like sunlight
5
Amidst falling snow,
a child's laughter warms the chill,
snowflakes pause to hear

Proud father with newborn child

Dad and me, Sopot 1956

1
Newborn's gentle breath,
father's pride shines in his eyes—
life's first tender bond
2
In the quiet dawn,
father holds his newborn close—
joy and pride entwined
3
Father's warm embrace,

tiny fingers grasp his own—
new life's soft promise
4
Under soft moonlight,
father's gaze meets newborn's eyes—
love's pure dawn unfolds
5
In the early light,
father beams with newborn's grace—
a world's new beginning

A rusted barn

1
Rusted barn stands still—
weathered walls and silent beams,
time's soft embrace lingers
2
In twilight's soft light,
rusted barn and setting sun,
shadows merge with dusk
3
Old barn in the field,
rusted roof beneath the stars,
echoes of the past
4
Autumn leaves drift down,
settling on the rusted barn,
seasons weave their tale
5
Under stormy skies,
rusted barn endures the gale,
stories in its rust

An ancient statue

1
Ancient statue's gaze—
weathered stone and time's embrace,
stillness holds its breath
2
In moonlight's soft glow,
ancient statue whispers old,
secrets of the past
3
Beneath the old tree,
ancient statue's silent watch,
shadows drift with time
4
Moss-clad and serene,
ancient statue in the mist,
echoes of the past
5
Sunrise on cold stone,
ancient statue greets the dawn,
silence greets the light

A goldfish pond

1
Goldfish glide through dusk—
ripples trace the pond's stillness,
moonlight's gentle touch
2
In the pond's calm blue,
goldfish weave through shadows soft,
lilies sway with grace
3
Morning light reflects
in the goldfish pond's clear depths,
dreams ripple and fade
4
Stillness on the pond—
goldfish flicker in the shade,
leaves drift on the breeze
5
Beneath the still pond,
goldfish stir in liquid gold,
whispers of the deep

A butterfly landing

1
Butterfly alights—
a whisper on the petal,
stillness in its grace
2
Gentle wings descend,
butterfly lands softly here,
breath of springtime's touch
3
In morning's soft light,
butterfly lands with quiet,
flowers hold their breath
4
On a silent bloom,
butterfly rests for a while,
time pauses with grace
5
Flutter of soft wings,
butterfly lands on the leaf,
shadows dance with joy

The echo of a bell

1
Bell's echo fades slow—
mountain shadows stretch and yawn,
silence wraps the dusk
2
In evening's soft hush,
bell's echo drifts through the mist,
whispers from the past
3
Under moonlit sky,
bell's echo weaves through the night,
stars listen in peace
4
Temple bell's clear ring,
echoes through the forest deep,
time's soft reverberance
5
Distant bell's clear chime,
echoes linger in the breeze,
moments drift away

A desert sunset

1
Desert sunset glows—
sand dunes bathed in warming light,
day's last breath of fire
2
In the still, hot dusk,
sun sinks behind the dunes' curve,
shadows stretch and fade
3
Crimson sky turns gold,
desert's vastness calms to dusk,
whispers of the heat
4
Sunset over sand,
colors blend in quiet waves,
night enfolds the dunes
5
Desert evening cools,
sunset spills its final light,
stars blink into view

A quiet evening

1
Quiet evening falls—
a single star softly glows,
whispers of the dusk
2
In twilight's soft hush,
crickets sing their evening song,
shadows deepen still
3
Evening's calm descends,
the moon bathes the world in light,
peace wraps the still night
4
Under calm night skies,
a breeze stirs the quiet trees,
darkness holds its breath
5
Softly fading light,
evening's calm enfolds the world,
stars awaken slow

The sound of the ocean

1
Ocean's rhythm sings—
waves crash on the moonlit shore,
whispers of the deep
2
Endless ocean hums,
waves crash and seagulls call out,
echoes in the breeze
3
In twilight's soft hush,
ocean's voice rolls low and deep,
night embraces sound
4
Waves caress the sand,
ocean's roar fades to a sigh,
dusk swallows the tide
5
Moonlight on the waves,
ocean's endless murmurs reach,
night's deep lullaby

A wooden canoe

1
Wooden canoe drifts—
whispers of the still lake's breath,
silence on the waves
2
In morning's soft mist,
wooden canoe glides gently,
leaves tremble in wake
3
On the quiet lake,
a wooden canoe rocks slow,
sunlight paints the ripples
4
Ancient wood afloat,
canoe carved by patient hands,
stillness meets the dawn
5
Evening's soft hues blend,
wooden canoe drifts away,
moonlight cradles it

A fallen leaf

1
Crimson whispers fall,
autumn's breath on the cool breeze—
a leaf's last descent
2
Silent forest floor,
a lone leaf twirls to its rest—
stillness in its wake
3
Fallen leaf, so still,
one with twilight's quiet hues—
season's gentle end
4
Drifting through the dusk,
a single leaf's journey ends—
moonlight on the path
5
Wind's gentle caress,
a leaf dances to its rest—
nature's fleeting grace

The scent of rain on earth

1
Earth breathes, rain returns—
the scent of fresh earth rises,
whispers through the leaves
2
Summer rain descends,
soil awakens with its scent—
a quiet rebirth
3
Petals drink the rain,
earth's fragrance rises anew—
sweetness fills the air
4
Morning mist and rain,
earth's aroma greets the dawn—
life's soft, fragrant touch
5
Rain's gentle embrace,
earth exudes its deep perfume—
a symphony of scents

A winter's night sky

1
Winter's night sky cold,
stars pierce through the velvet dark—
silence whispers still
2
Frost on the window,
a moon floats in stillness—
night's breath, serene
3
Crystal night above,
constellations softly freeze—
a breath of winter
4
Snowflakes drift and fade,
the sky's soft, unbroken blue—
winter's quiet dome
5
Barren trees below,
stars shimmer through the still air—
winter's night unfolds

A summer thunderstorm

1
Summer storm rolls in,
thunder rumbles through the heat—
rain's fierce, cooling kiss
2
Lightning splits the sky,
a brief flash of summer's rage—
rain drums on the roof
3
Warm wind meets the rain,
thunder's growl and lightning's flash—
summer's wild embrace
4
Dark clouds gather close,
the storm's voice rumbles and roars—
rain sweeps through the dusk
5
Lightning paints the night,
a summer storm's fierce display—
cool relief arrives

A star-filled sky

1
A sea of night stars,
whispers of eternity—
silence draped in light
2
Stars scatter the dark,
each a distant, quiet flame—
night's vast tapestry
3
Stillness fills the sky,
a quilt of countless pinpricks—
night's endless embrace
4
Moonlight softly fades,
stars emerge in gentle waves—
night's jeweled cloak
5
Celestial gleam,
the night sky's silent chorus—
dreams drift among stars

A strong, proud grandfather

My grandfather Jacob 1970

1
Strong hands lift the child,
grandfather's proud smile beams—
legacy in joy
2
In the autumn light,
grandfather's sturdy arms—
young boy's hero's gaze
3

On a grassy hill,
grandfather's laughter rings—
boy's world grows strong, bright
4
Beneath ancient trees,
grandfather's pride and strength—
young boy's bright eyes shine
5
Grandfather's deep voice,
boy's laughter fills the old hands—
generations meet

A moss-covered rock

1
Ancient rock adorned,
moss cloaks its timeworn surface—
green whispers of age
‘

2
Moss upon the stone,
softened by the years' embrace—
a silent green tale
‘

3
In the forest’s shade,
a moss-covered rock sleeps deep—
time’s quiet canvas
‘

4
Green tapestry forms,
moss weaves over the cold stone—
nature’s gentle touch
‘

5
On the mossy stone,
sunlight filters through the leaves—
a moment of calm

An abandoned house

1
Dusty shadows linger,
an abandoned house sighs low—
echoes of the past
2
Once a home now still,
windows gaze with empty eyes—
silence wraps the walls
3
Overgrown with vines,
the old house dreams of the past—
nature's soft embrace
4
Creaks through empty halls,
the wind whispers through broken panes—
time's gentle caress
5
Moonlight through the eaves,
an abandoned house sleeps on—
memories drift by

A field of snowdrops

1
Field of snowdrops blooms,
white petals pierce winter's veil—
spring whispers through frost
2
Snowdrops in the field,
a soft breath of winter's end—
hope beneath the snow
3
White blooms on the snow,
a promise of spring's return—
fragile yet so bright
4
In the cold still air,
snowdrops rise from winter's grasp—
spring's first gentle touch
5
Scattered snowdrops sway,
a quiet dance in the cold—
winter's soft farewell

A secluded garden

1
Hidden garden sleeps,
whispers of leaves in still air—
peaceful solitude
2
In a quiet nook,
a secluded garden breathes—
time's gentle retreat
3
Hidden blooms await,
sunlight filters through the walls—
serenity's touch
4
In the shaded cool,
a secluded garden dreams—
soft petals, silent
5
Secret garden rests,
crickets sing in twilight's hush—
solitude in bloom

A gossamer spiderweb

1
Gossamer threads glint,
a spider's delicate lace—
morning dew's embrace
2
In dawn's soft light,
a spider's web sparkles clear—
fragile artistry
3
Web of silver strands,
woven in morning mist—
nature's fleeting thread
4
In the cool still air,
a gossamer web trembles—
a breath of dawn's grace
5
Delicate and fine,
a spider's web holds the dawn—
silken whispers shine

A wind-swept meadow

1
Waves across the field,
wind sweeps through the meadow's grass—
whispers on the breeze
2
In the open space,
wind dances through the tall grass—
a meadow's soft song
3
Wind-kissed meadow sways,
grass bends in a graceful sweep—
nature's quiet dance
4
Under endless sky,
a wind-swept meadow breathes deep—
whispers on the wind
5
Grass ripples like sea,
wind weaves through the meadow wide—
a silent symphony

A full moon rising

1
Full moon climbs the sky,
silver rising through the dusk—
night's gentle lantern
2
Moon ascends the dark,
a full orb in quiet grace—
night's serene beacon
3
In the velvet night,
a full moon rises slowly—
silent brilliance blooms
4
Rising through the trees,
a full moon's soft glow reveals—
whispers of the night
5
Full moon's gentle rise,
illuminates the still world—
night's calm embrace shines

A fresh snowfall on trees

1
Snow drapes the bare trees,
a quilt of winter's white—
silence wraps the branches
2
Winter's gentle touch,
fresh snow blankets the dark woods—
trees in soft embrace
3
Snowfall on the boughs,
each branch holds a pure snowfall—
winter's quiet gift
4
In the still of dawn,
fresh snow adorns the bare trees—
a tranquil, white scene
5
Branches bowed with snow,
a fresh blanket softly falls—
winter's calm stillness

A peaceful pond

1
Still pond mirrors sky,
ripples dance with gentle grace—
silence holds the scene
2
A peaceful pond rests,
reflecting sky and tall trees—
stillness in the depths
3
Moonlight on the pond,
soft ripples stir the stillness—
night's serene embrace
4
Dragonflies at rest,
hovering above the calm—
peace upon the pond
5
In the quiet dusk,
a pond's surface, glassy smooth—
tranquility holds

An autumn harvest

1
Autumn's golden yield,
fields heavy with ripened grain—
harvest moonlight glows
2
Baskets brim with fruit,
autumn's bounty fills the air—
leaves fall in whispers
3
Crimson apples gleam,
sunset warms the gathered crop—
autumn's tender touch
4
Harvest wind stirs leaves,
grain ripples in the cool dusk—
season's quiet gift
5
In the fading light,
autumn's harvest laid bare—
earth's final embrace

A flickering lantern

1
Flickering lantern,
its light dances in the night—
shadows softly sway
2
In the evening chill,
a lantern's wavering glow—
whispers through the dark
3
Lantern's light falters,
casting gentle, trembling beams—
night's warm breath flickers
4
In the quiet dark,
a lantern's light sways softly—
night's tender embrace
5
In the still of night,
a lantern's fleeting glow sways—
soft whispers of light

A morning dew

1
Morning dew drapes leaves,
tiny pearls on silken threads—
daybreak's quiet gift
2
Dew upon the grass,
a delicate shimmer glows—
morning's soft embrace
3
In dawn's soft light,
dew beads on a spider's web—
nature's fragile art
4
Coolness of the dawn,
dew drops on the waking field—
day's first gentle breath
5
Morning dew adorns,
each blade of grass a jewel—
silence in the light

A serene lake at dusk

1
Dusk settles on lake,
a mirror of fading light—
serenity's veil
2
Still lake at twilight,
mountains darken, sky softens—
night's quiet reflection
3
Evening whispers low,
a serene lake in deep calm—
shadows gently blend
4
Dusk's brush on the lake,
a still surface in twilight—
peace in shadows' hold
5
In the dimming light,
the lake's surface smooth and calm—
day's gentle farewell

The buzz of a bee

1
In summer's heat,
a bee's soft buzz through the blooms—
nature's gentle hum
2
Buzz of a lone bee,
dancing from bloom to bloom—
summer's quiet song
3
In the sunlit field,
a bee's buzz weaves through the blooms—
summer's fleeting thread
4
Among the flowers,
a bee's steady hum persists—
life in gentle flight
5
Buzz drifts through the air,
a bee's rhythm in the blooms—
summer's fleeting dance

A quiet snowfall

1
Silent snow descends,
whispers on the sleeping earth—
winter's quiet shroud
2
Snowflakes drift in peace,
covering the world in white—
stillness fills the air
3
In the gentle dusk,
snow falls softly on the streets—
a hush blankets all
4
Snowfall's tender touch,
silence wraps the trees and ground—
winter's soft embrace
5
Quiet flakes descend,
blanketing the world in white—
winter's calm whisper

An old lighthouse

1
Old lighthouse stands firm,
weathered by the sea's embrace—
beacon in the mist
2
Worn by wind and time,
the lighthouse guards the quiet shore—
its light pierces dusk
3
Ancient tower glows,
guiding through the stormy night—
wisdom in the light
4
Silent lighthouse beams,
its shadow etched in twilight—
a sentinel's grace
5
Lighthouse by the sea,
waves crash against weathered stone—
time's steadfast guide

A marriage made in heaven

Mum and Dad's wedding 1955 Poland

1
Under twilight's glow,
vows whispered beneath the stars—
heaven's gentle grace
2
In the evening's hush,

two hearts merge beneath soft light—
heaven's pure embrace
3
As the day fades out,
joy sparkles in the night air—
love's celestial bond
4
In the moon's soft light,
two souls unite with a smile—
heaven's perfect dance
5
Hand in hand they stand,
beneath the sky's warm blessing—
love's eternal link

The scent of fresh bread

1
Warmth from the oven,
fresh bread's scent fills the kitchen—
comfort in the air
2
Morning's first embrace,
the aroma of fresh bread—
day's gentle whisper
3
Bread's warm fragrance drifts,
a hint of crust and soft inside—
home's welcoming scent
4
In the quiet dawn,
the scent of fresh-baked bread wafts—
a promise of warmth
5
Crust and soft inside,
fresh bread's aroma lingers—
simple morning joy

A soft breeze on the beach

1
Soft breeze on the beach,
waves caress the golden shore—
whispers in the sand
2
Gentle sea breeze sighs,
drifting over sunlit waves—
beach's cool, soft breath
3
On the sandy shore,
a soft breeze stirs the sea spray—
day's tender caress
4
Breeze whispers through dunes,
softly sweeping over sand—
ocean's quiet breath
5
Beach breeze lightly blows,
waves ripple under sunlight—
summer's soft embrace

A crisp autumn breeze

1
Crisp autumn breeze sweeps,
leaves tumble in golden dance—
whispers of the fall
2
In the autumn air,
a crisp breeze stirs fallen leaves—
season's sharp embrace
3
Cool breeze through the trees,
autumn's breath rustles the leaves—
a crisp, fleeting touch
4
Autumn's crisp exhale,
leaves flutter in the brisk wind—
day's clear, cool embrace
5
Crisp breeze on the field,
whispers through the amber grass—
autumn's gentle chill

A gentle snowfall

1
Gentle snow descends,
flakes drift on a quiet breeze—
whispers of stillness
2
Soft snowflakes descend,
blanketing the world in white—
silence fills the air
3
Snowfall's gentle touch,
each flake lands with tender grace—
winter's hush unfolds
4
In the soft snowfall,
a tranquil world is revealed—
peace in every flake
5
Lightly falling snow,
a soft hush over the earth—
winter's gentle breath

The rhythm of waves

1
Rhythm of the waves,
their pulse against the sandy shore—
ocean's timeless song
2
Waves break with a hush,
rhythm flows in endless dance—
sea's eternal beat
3
In the moonlit night,
waves whisper their steady rhythm—
a lullaby's call
4
Tide's soft, rolling song,
waves caress the quiet shore—
nature's gentle beat
5
Waves in rhythmic sweep,
ocean's breath in constant flow—
time's undying pulse

A leaf drifting in water

1
A leaf drifts in calm,
gently floating on the pond—
autumn's quiet grace
2
Leaf on still water,
drifting in the sunlit pool—
nature's soft embrace
3
On the pond's smooth face,
a single leaf drifts slowly—
time's tranquil journey
4
Leaf rides the water,
dancing with the ripples' flow—
serenity's drift
5
In the quiet pond,
a leaf glides through stillness—
moment's fleeting peace

The call of an owl

1
Owl's call pierces night,
echoes through the silent woods—
moon's soft, watchful eye
2
In the quiet dark,
an owl's call breaks the stillness—
whispers through the trees
3
Night's deep silence holds,
an owl's call drifts on the breeze—
solitude's soft voice
4
Under moon's pale light,
an owl's call drifts on the breeze—
night's lonely refrain
5
Owl's call in the dark,
haunting through the forest's hush—
night's ancient rhythm

A warm summer night

1
Warm summer night's breath,
crickets sing beneath the stars—
moonlight's gentle kiss
2
Night's warm embrace holds,
fireflies dance in the dark—
summer's quiet hum
3
Under summer's heat,
the night air softens with stars—
a world wrapped in warmth
4
Summer night's warm glow,
whispers of the day still linger—
peace in the stillness
5
In the warm night air,
jasmine's scent drifts slowly by—
summer's tender sigh

A misty valley

1
Misty valley wakes,
fog cloaks the silent hillsides—
whispers in the haze
2
In the misty vale,
mountains blend with drifting fog—
a world veiled in gray
3
Valley draped in mist,
soft outlines of distant peaks—
day's quiet shroud falls
4
Morning mist enfolds,
valley swathed in gauzy white—
silence deepens still
5
Fog drifts through the vale,
valley's breath in soft embrace—
dreams within the mist

The glint of sunlight on snow

1
Sunlight on the snow,
glints like scattered diamond dust—
winter's fleeting gleam
2
Snow sparkles in light,
sun's touch on a crystal world—
a moment's bright flash
3
Sunlit snowflakes shine,
each flake a tiny prism—
day's soft, bright whisper
4
Glinting on the snow,
sunlight dances in the cold—
winter's bright touch
5
Sunlight on fresh snow,
a fleeting, sparkling glow—
winter's fleeting grace

A mountain waterfall

1
Mountain waterfall,
cascades through ancient granite—
song of the high peaks
2
Waterfall descends,
crystal veil in mountain shade—
echoes in the mist
3
From the mountain's crest,
a waterfall's silver thread—
whispers through the pines
4
Falls from rugged heights,
splashing into the cool pool—
nature's quiet roar
5
In the mountain's heart,
a waterfall's endless fall—
time's cascading grace

A fresh spring rain

1
Fresh spring rain descends,
whispers to the waking earth—
buds unfurl in joy
2
Spring rain gently falls,
nourishing the tender shoots—
earth's soft, green rebirth
3
Raindrops kiss the leaves,
spring's gentle tears grace the ground—
nature's quiet song
4
In the springtime rain,
petrichor fills the cool air—
a new season wakes
5
Soft spring rain renews,
drumming on the leafy canopy—
life's tender embrace

A cozy blanket

1
Under soft blanket,
warmth wraps the quiet evening—
night's gentle embrace
2
A cozy blanket,
folded warmth against the cold—
home's soft refuge waits
3
Blanket draped in hush,
cradles in the still night air—
dreams wrapped in its warmth
4
In the evening's calm,
a blanket's tender embrace—
winter's gentle hold
5
Cozy blanket folds,
sheltering from winter's bite—
peace in its embrace

Mother and boy at the zoo

Mother and Alex at the zoo Poland, 1957

1
Mother's guiding hand,
young boy's eyes wide with wonder—
zoo's world unfolds slow
2
At the bears' soft play,
mother and boy's laughter blend—
wildlife's gentle call
3
Giraffes' graceful necks,
young boy's gaze meets mother's smile—
zoo's quiet marvels
4
In the aviary,
mother and son watch birds soar—

joy in feathered flight

5

Elephant's slow tread,
mother and boy share a hush—
nature's grand parade

A bright autumn day

1
Autumn sun warms the field,
crimson leaves drift in bright light—
day's vivid embrace
2
On a clear autumn day,
golden hues paint the still air—
peace in every leaf
3
Bright autumn sky smiles,
trees aflame with fiery tones—
day's crisp, brilliant touch
4
In the autumn light,
bright leaves flutter in the breeze—
day's golden whisper
5
Under autumn's sun,
the world glows in vivid hues—
day's clear, warm canvas

A calm sea at dawn

1
Dawn breaks on still seas,
gentle waves kiss the quiet shore—
morning's tranquil breath
2
Calm sea at dawn's edge,
soft light caresses the waves—
day's first whispered peace
3
At dawn, the calm sea,
reflects the blush of the sky—
serenity's touch
4
Morning sea in peace,
horizon meets the soft light—
dawn's quiet embrace
5
Dawn on a calm sea,
gentle ripples meet the light—
a new day's soft sigh

The glow of fireflies

1
Fireflies at dusk,
glow like stars in summer's veil—
night's gentle lanterns
2
In the evening hush,
fireflies flicker softly—
whispers of the dark
3
Glow of fireflies dance,
scattered stars on summer's breath—
night's fleeting embrace
4
Summer night aglow,
fireflies weave through the dark—
magic in their flight
5
In twilight's soft glow,
fireflies trace the still air—
light's fleeting ballet

A young boy enjoying the snow

Zakopane, Poland 1959

1
Snowflakes kiss his cheeks,
young boy's laughter fills the air—
winter's joyful dance
2
Footprints in fresh snow,
young boy's hands shape icy dreams—
winter's play unfolds
3
Snowy fields of white,
young boy's sled glides down the hill—
joy in every sweep
4
In the frosty light,
young boy's snowball fight begins—

cold day's warm delight

5

Snow-draped trees and hills,
young boy twirls in frosty air—
winter's pure delight

A quiet snowfall at night

1
Snowfall gently drifts,
young boy watches through the pane—
night's soft, silent cloak
2
In quiet dusk,
young boy's breath fogs up the glass—
flakes dance in moonlight
3
Silent snow descends,
young boy's eyes wide with wonder—
night enfolds in white
4
Under starlit skies,
young boy tracks each falling flake—
winter's whispered peace
5
Snow blankets the world,
young boy dreams in stillness—
night's pure, silent grace

The rustling of leaves

1
Rustling leaves whisper,
footsteps through the autumn woods—
nature's soft embrace
2
Leaves dance in the breeze,
laughter joins the woodland song—
autumn's fleeting joy
3
Under leafy shade,
a hand brushes the soft ground—
whispers of the wind
4
In the forest still,
leaves murmur in the soft breeze—
secrets in their rustle
5
Sunlight through the trees,
gaze follows each drifting leaf—
fall's gentle murmur

The chirping of birds at dawn

1
At dawn's first light,
chirping birds weave morning's song—
daybreak's gentle call
2
In the still dawn air,
birdsong pierces through the hush—
new day softly wakes
3
Morning's quiet breaks,
chirping birds in sunlight's glow—
whispers of the day
4
Sunrise paints the sky,
birds sing out in clear, crisp notes—
dawn's serenade begins
5
Dew on the soft grass,
chirping birds announce the day—
nature's gentle nudge

A starry night sky

1
Stars pierce the dark veil,
whispers in the still night sky—
silence glitters bright
2
Under starry quilt,
a breeze hums through the quiet—
night's soft, distant light
3
Celestial frost,
stars scattered in velvet blue—
night's deep, tranquil breath
4
Moon's glow softly fades,
stars emerge in endless blue—
whispers of the night
5
In the vast night sky,
constellations softly pulse—
a quiet, endless dance

The silence of a forest

1
In the forest hush,
stillness deepens, shadows blend—
whispers of the trees
2
Silent ancient pines,
moss blankets the forest floor—
breath of timeless peace
3
Soft light through the leaves,
the forest holds its quiet—
nature’s calm embrace
4
Between the tall trees,
a breeze pauses, then resumes—
forest's breath so still
5
In the deep forest,
every sound seems far away—
silence fills the air

A single rose

1
In morning's soft light,
a single rose stands alone—
dew on crimson petals
2
Under the still sky,
one rose whispers summer's end—
fragile, bold, and lone
3
Amidst green leaves,
a solitary rose blooms—
a silent farewell
4
One rose in the dusk,
its fragrance drifts on the breeze—
night embraces it
5
In the quiet garden,
a single rose unfolds—
a moment's grace lingers

Mother sitting with flowers

1
In the garden's calm,
mother among the blossoms—
petals and soft smiles
2
Beneath flowering trees,
mother rests in quiet shade—

fragrance fills the air
3
Bright blooms at her feet,
laughter mingles with the breeze—
spring's gentle embrace
4
Amidst wild blooms,
her hand brushes petals soft—
nature's tender touch
5
In the garden's heart,
mother watches petals fall—
season's quiet grace

A cup of hot cocoa

1
Steam rises softly,
a cup of cocoa warms—
winter's gentle hug
2
Crimson mug held close,
rich aroma fills the air—
comfort in each sip
3
Snowflakes drift outside,
inside, cocoa's warmth blooms—
evening's sweet reprieve
4
Chocolaty steam
drifts in the cold, quiet room—
heart finds its solace
5
In the still of dusk,
a cup of cocoa glows warm—
night's cozy embrace

The sound of distant thunder

1
Distant thunder rumbles—
sky whispers of rain to come,
earth holds its breath still
2
Clouds darken, low growls,
a solitary flash stirs—
distant thunder's call
3
Through the silent dusk,
a rumble breaks the stillness—
thunder's voice echoes
4
Far-off thunder rolls,
quiet night holds its rumble—
sky's deep murmuring
5
In twilight's hush,
distant thunder softly roars—
nature's deep murmur

A cat in the sun

1
Sunlit fur gleams—
a cat sprawls in warm rays,
dreaming in the light
2
In the sunbeam's pool,
a cat purrs, content and still—
afternoon's calm peace
3
Warmth on velvet paws,
a cat naps in golden light—
shadows softly shift
4
Sunlight filters in,
a cat basks in its embrace—
stillness fills the room
5
Sun through the window,
a cat stretches, slow and long—
day's gentle caress

A field of sunflowers

1
Sunflowers face east,
golden heads follow the sun—
warmth in every bloom
2
Field of golden suns,
sunflowers stretch to the sky—
summer's whispered song
3
Petals dance in light,
a field of sunflowers sways—
wind's soft, golden touch
4
Sunflowers reach high,
each head a bright, sunlit crown—
day's steadfast embrace
5
In sun's golden gaze,
sunflowers bow and whisper—
nature's quiet praise

A drifting autumn leaf

1
Autumn leaf descends,
caught in the quiet breeze's
dance through fading light
2
A lone leaf spirals
through the cool, crisp breath of fall—
whispers of the year
3
Golden leaf drifts down,
carried on the autumn breeze—
season's gentle sigh
4
In the still park,
an autumn leaf floats slowly—
a whisper of change
5
Leaf on the wind drifts,
floating from its golden branch—
autumn's soft caress

A morning mist over the lake

1
Mist drapes the still lake—
dawn's first light breaks through soft veil,
whispers of morning
2
Morning mist ascends,
lake's edge hidden in gray veil—
silence meets the sky
3
Soft mist hugs the lake,
water's edge lost in fog's drift—
day stirs from the shroud
4
Mist lifts from still lake,
water's edge blurred in gentle—
morning's quiet breath
5
Fog swirls on still lake,
dawn's light brushes the water—
secrets in the mist

The scent of autumn leaves

1
Crisp leaves underfoot—
autumn's scent in cool, still air,
whispers of the past
2
Red and gold cascade,
earth breathes out its autumn smell—
season's fleeting kiss
3
Wind scatters dry leaves,
scent of fall fills quiet woods—
rustling memories
4
Underfoot they crack,
autumn's perfume in the dusk—
earth's old, sweet secret
5
In the forest's hush,
scent of leaves in twilight still—
autumn's tender breath

A quiet snowfall on a city street

1
Snowflakes gently fall,
city lights blur through the hush—
winter's silent touch
2
Soft flakes drift, unseen,
urban streets in quiet grace—
winter's quiet breath
3
Snow mutes the city,
footsteps vanish in the white—
stillness wraps the street
4
Snow descends in peace,
city noise wrapped in white veils—
whispers of the cold
5
Pure white veil descends,
city shapes in quiet blur—
snow's gentle embrace

The glow of the setting sun

1
Sun dips below hills,
a blush of warmth fades to night—
day's final whisper
2
Setting sun's last glow,
clouds painted in fiery hues—
night unfurls its cloak
3
Golden light retreats,
twilight's soft touch lingers on—
shadows stretch and yawn
4
Crimson strokes the sky,
sunset's fire whispers to dusk—
night's cool breath arrives
5
Evening's warm kiss,
sun sinks beneath the horizon—
day yields to the night

About Alex Telman

Alex Telman is a globally recognized spiritual healer, author, and one of the country's most read poets. With over 45 years of experience, he has dedicated his life to helping individuals break free from negative energies, trauma, and spiritual blockages. His transformative work has empowered a diverse range of clients, including celebrities, business leaders, educators, and everyday individuals, guiding them toward emotional well-being, personal growth, and spiritual fulfillment.

ALEX TELMAN

From an early age, Alex demonstrated extraordinary abilities to perceive and remove harmful energies and entities, a gift that first emerged when he was just three years old. This rare talent led him to study with psychic masters across the globe—Afghanistan, France, Sweden, Israel, England, and Australia—each recognizing his unique gifts and helping him refine his craft.

In addition to his healing practice, Alex has practiced as a barrister, teacher, university lecturer, and small business owner, offering a well-rounded perspective on healing that combines spirituality with practical action. He is also an accomplished author, whose writings inspire and uplift readers by exploring the depths of human emotion and the power of self-healing.

Through his sessions, Alex has helped countless individuals overcome emotional turmoil and reclaim their lives. His work transcends cultural and geographical boundaries, offering profound healing to those in need. His mission is simple yet powerful: to guide people back to their authentic selves, helping them live with purpose, peace, and fulfillment.

With a career built on compassion, wisdom, and deep spiritual insight, Alex remains a beacon of hope for anyone seeking to overcome their struggles and wanting to step into a life of clarity and joy.

Other Titles by Alex Telman

Non Fiction

Think Like a Modern Guru
Mindshift: Change Your Life in 4 Days
Mastering Hypnosis: Complete Step-by-Step Manual, Case Studies, and Sample Scripts
From Cursed to Cured: 100 True Stories of Healing from Curses
Connecting to the Afterlife: a how-to guide
Your Journey from Death to Rebirth
Empower Your Sundays: Unlocking Inner Strength for a Resilient Life
The Truth Behind the Creation Story: A Journey Through Reincarnation
Practical Mentalism in a Nutshell
Reprogram Your Mind in a Nutshell
Meditation in a Nutshell
Alex Telman in Quotes

Novels

Down and Out in Byron Bay
One Life, Half Lived
God Speaks: A Journey Through Creation in His Own Words
Jesus Speaks: The Man Behind the Miracle in His Own Words

Poetry

Echoes of September 11
Homeless in New York
Burning Echoes of Time
From Dawn to Dusk: the life cycle in sonnets

Eternal Echoes: The Tapestry of Time and the Unseen
Snapshots of People I Have Never Met
Legends and Lessons: 36 Myths Unveiled
A Measure of Time: The Eternal Voyage of Self
Ashes of Verses: Poems Burned But Not Forgotten
Reflections on Solitude: A Poetic Journey Through The Lonely Mind
Your Friendship is a Museum
Whispers to Bella

www.ingramcontent.com/pod-product-compliance
Lightning Source LLC
LaVergne TN
LVHW010109170826
845678LV00012B/2307

* 9 7 9 8 2 3 0 7 3 1 1 1 5 *